And Then I Let Go

–Kashish Agrahari

Connect with the author:
Instagram: @miss.peace91

For that smile
you lost...

and for the day
you find it again.

While trying to be there for everyone,
did you forget to be there for yourself?

Have you ever had someone
you could talk to for hours,
and still not feel tired?

Someone who felt like peace,
in the middle of all your chaos?

Have you ever cried on your bathroom floor?

That anxiety...
that pain...
those shaking hands...
have you ever felt it?

You talked to me
like nothing had ever changed.

There was no distance,
no silence between us.

You smiled,
and for a moment,
everything felt right again.

I didn't feel confused anymore.
I didn't feel like I was losing you.

It felt easy...
like it used to.

And just when I started believing it was real

I opened my eyes.

I didn't realize when things started changing.

Maybe it was slow,
or maybe I just didn't want to see it.

All I knew was,
something that once felt right...
no longer felt the same.

I tried so hard to ignore it.

I kept telling myself
that it was just a phase,
that everything would be okay again.

But somewhere deep down,
I knew something had changed.

You were still there,
but not the same.

And somehow,
that hurt more
than your absence ever could.

It wasn't sudden.

It was the small things.

The late replies.
The shorter conversations.
The pauses that used to feel warm... now felt heavy.

I noticed everything,
even when I pretended not to.

And somewhere in between all of this,
it became clear...

It's funny how a stranger
can become the reason
you keep checking your phone
a hundred times a day...

waiting for something
that may never come.

And then came the *overthinking*.

Every message replayed in my head
like a broken record.

Did I say something wrong?
Did I become less important?
Or was I just imagining everything?

I started reading between lines
that probably never existed.

Every *"seen"* felt heavier than silence.

And every notification
made my heart jump...
just to fall again.

Where did it all go?

The way you used to care about every small thing...
the way you would get annoyed just to talk to me...
the way you always found reasons to be around me...

Where did that version of you disappear?

"What hurts more than losing someone...
is watching them change in front of you."

It all happened so suddenly...

I didn't even realize when it started becoming a part of my life.

I still remember everything
our first talk it was October 2024,
you in that *red and black check shirt with your curly hair,*
and your simple "Hello" that meant nothing to you...

but everything to me.

I remember it all...

but maybe I'm the only one who still remembers it all

I started noticing the distance
in ways I couldn't explain.

It wasn't just in your words,
it was in the way you said them.

You were there...
but it felt like you weren't.

And I kept asking myself,
was it always like this,
and I just didn't see it?

Or did you really change...
and I was the only one left behind?

"It's confusing when someone makes you feel special one day... and invisible the next."

You didn’t leave all at once...
you left in pieces,

I kept hoping
you’d notice the distance...

but you were the one
creating it.

I sometimes imagine us
in a different version of reality.

Where you never changed.
Where I never had to question
what we were.

In that version,
you still look at me
the way you used to.

You still choose me,
without hesitation.

And I don't have to pretend
that everything is okay...
because it actually is.

But then I blink,
and I'm back here

where nothing feels the same,
and you feel like someon
I never really knew.

I still remember that day.
You said it so easily...

*"If she ever comes back,
I'll go back to her."*
You didn't hesitate.
You didn't even think twice.
And I stood there,
smiling like it didn't hurt
Like I was strong enough
to hear that
and still stay.
Maybe I thought
you'd choose me anyway.
Maybe I believed
I was enough to make you stay.
But the truth is...
you were never mine to keep.

*I was just someone
you stayed with...*
until she came back.

I don't hold anything against you anymore. Maybe things were never meant to stay the way I wanted them to, and I've slowly learned to accept that. I genuinely hope you find the kind of love that feels easy, the kind that doesn't leave you confused or questioning your place in someone's life. I hope someone understands you in ways I tried to, and gives you the comfort you were always looking for. Wherever life takes you, I hope it brings you peace and happiness. *And even if we were never meant to last, I'm still grateful for what we once had.* I just hope life is kinder to you, and that you become everything you once dreamed of.

Maybe some stories are not meant to last forever. Maybe they come into our lives just to teach us something we didn't know we needed to learn. For the longest time, I kept searching for answers, trying to understand where it all went wrong. But now, I'm slowly realizing that not everything has an explanation. Some things just end, quietly, without giving you the closure you thought you needed. And maybe that's okay. *Maybe the real lesson was never about holding on, but about learning when to let go and choosing yourself, even when it hurts.*

(Take your time dear,
you don't have to rush your healing.)

Maybe some things in life are never meant to be ours, no matter how deeply we wish for them. Like a child whispering prayers into the night for parents who will never return, or like waiting for the sun in a sky that has already chosen darkness. Sometimes it feels like writing letters to an address that no longer exists, or holding onto a song that has already reached its last note. And sometimes, it feels like that last leaf on a dying tree holding on, even when everything else has already fallen, giving hope that life is still there, even when it's slowly fading away. Like standing at a closed door, hoping it might open if you wait a little longer, or chasing a train that disappeared long before you even arrived. I think loving you felt a lot like that like believing in something with your whole heart, even when every sign quietly told you it would never be yours. And maybe the hardest part isn't letting go, but accepting that some things were never meant to stay, no matter how much they meant to you.

If this feels a little too close to your heart, I want you to know that it's okay to pause here. You don't have to carry everything at once. Some pain is like a storm it feels endless when you're in it, but even the darkest storms eventually pass, leaving behind a sky that slowly learns to be clear again. And you, you are not the broken pieces you're holding right now. *You are more like that last leaf on a tired tree,* still holding on, still surviving, even when everything around you feels like it's falling apart. *So if your eyes are heavy with tears, let them fall. Healing doesn't come from pretending you're fine;* it comes from allowing yourself to feel, and then slowly, gently, finding your way back to yourself.

Some people
don't come into your life
to stay.
They come
when it's convenient for them.
They take
your time,
your care,
your effort...
and leave
once they're done.
And you keep thinking
it meant something.
But to them,

it was just
a phase.
Not everyone
who talks to you daily
is meant to stay.
Some people
just come
to feel less lonely...
and leave you
feeling the same.

Think of it like this you're standing at a station, waiting for a train you truly believe will come back. You keep looking down the tracks, hoping to hear that familiar sound again, convincing yourself that maybe it's just late, maybe it's on its way. But what you don't realize is that train already left a long time ago. And still, you stay there, holding on to the idea of its return. People pass by, time keeps moving, everything around you changes, yet you remain in the same place, waiting for something that isn't coming back. *So maybe it's not about how long you can wait, but about when you finally decide to leave the station yourself.*

Even when the world feels empty
and no one stands beside you...

remember,
I'm always here.

I remember everything. And still, every time I try to forget. But forgetting is not easy... I have to remember it all again. I have to remind myself how you chose not to talk, how you let go of my hand instead of holding it. I have to remember how you knew I cried every night, and still, you didn't come. I have to remember how you left so easily, like nothing mattered. How your care for me slowly ended... while I kept holding on. I have to remember every time I cried... just to tell myself that I need to forget you.

Healing didn't happen all at once.

It started with small things...
like not checking my phone again and again,
like not waiting for a message that never came.

Some days were still hard,
but they didn't feel as heavy as before.

I slowly started choosing myself,
even if it felt strange at first.

I am still not fully okay,
but I am better than I was.

And maybe,
that's enough for now.

I started taking care of myself again.

Doing the things I once loved,
without thinking of you.

At first, it felt empty...
like something was missing.

But slowly,
that empty space
started feeling like peace.

I realized
I don't need someone else
to feel complete.

I was always enough...

I just forgot it for a while.

Your memories
still cross my mind.

But now,
they don’t hurt
the same way.

For the first time,
I chose myself.

Not because I had to...
but because
I finally wanted to.

I stopped asking
why it happened.

Some things
don’t need answers
to be accepted.

I don't hate you anymore.

I just don't need you
the way I once did.

And maybe,
that's how I know...

I've finally moved on.

Somewhere in all of this,
I found a part of myself again.

The version of me
that smiled for no reason,
that didn't overthink everything,
that didn't wait for someone else
to feel okay.

I didn't lose myself completely...
I just forgot who I was.

It always started with
"just once."

Just one look,
just one check...

but it never stopped there.

I told myself
I was done.

But somehow,
I still found myself
checking your profile...

just to see
if anything had changed.

I don’t do it all the time anymore...

but sometimes,
without even thinking,
I still check.

Like my fingers
remember you
better than my mind.

Every time,
I tell myself...

this is the last time.

But somehow,
there's always
another "last time."

I don’t talk to you anymore.

But I still miss you...

Like touching a wound
just to check if it still hurts...
even when you already know
it does.

Like going back
to a place
you once called home...
even when
no one lives there anymore.

Like reading old chats
over and over again...
trying to find something
that was never there.

Like checking the door
again and again...
even when you know
no one is coming.

So maybe,
the first step isn't
forgetting you...

maybe it's
stopping myself
from going back.

I know I have stopped myself. I know I don't go back the way I used to. But sometimes... I still feel like checking again. Just once. Not because I expect anything... just because a part of me is still there. And maybe... it's okay to feel that way. Because somewhere, I also know you have someone now...
someone you chose.

And strangely,

I'm learning
to be okay with that too.

If you're still going back,
even after deciding not to...
don't be too hard on yourself.
Healing is not a straight path.
Some days,
you move forward...
and some days,
you find yourself
looking back again.
That doesn't mean
you're not healing.
It just means
you're human.
Just remember,
missing someone
doesn't mean
they belong in your life again.

And letting go
doesn't mean
you never cared.

If you feel this way,
you're not wrong.

It's not easy
to just forget someone
you once cared about.

Sometimes,
even after you stop,
a part of you
still goes back.

Not because you're weak...
but because you felt deeply.

And that's okay.

Just don't lose yourself
while holding on
to something
that is already gone.

You deserve
to move forward too.

At some point,
you have to be honest
with yourself.

Not everything
that felt right
was meant to stay.

And not everyone
who made you feel special
was meant to stay in your life.

You can miss them,
you can think about them…

but you don't have to
go back to them.

Because choosing yourself
is not wrong.

It's necessary.

If you still miss them,
it's okay.

It doesn't mean
you want them back.

It just means
you cared.

Don't go back
just because
it feels familiar.

Not everything
that feels right
is right for you.

Sometimes,
you have to choose
your peace...

even if your heart
still remembers them.

You don't have to
forget everything.

You just have to
stop going back to it.

Memories can stay...

but you don't have to
live in them.

Moving on
is not about
erasing someone.

It's about
choosing yourself
again and again.

One day,
you’ll stop checking.

It's Like chasing
a shadow...

the more you run,
the farther it goes.

Even if our paths cross again...

I won't turn back
this time.

And after that moment,
I'll keep walking...
like nothing happened.

But later,
when I'm alone,

it will all come back.

The memories,
the feelings,
the way everything once felt.

Not as heavy as before...
but not completely gone either.

I won't cry
the way I used to...
but I won't be
completely untouched.
Maybe that's what healing looks like
you don't break anymore...

but you still feel
a little.

There are so many things
I wanted to say to you...

but I never did.

Not because
I didn't feel them...

but because
I knew
you wouldn't understand.

I wanted to tell you
how much you meant to me.

Not in big words...
just in the small things
I did for you every day.

I wanted to tell you
how much it hurt
when you started changing.

How I noticed everything...
even the things
you thought I didn't.

I wanted to ask you
so many questions...

but I stayed quiet.

Because somewhere,
I already knew
the answers
would hurt more.

I don't notice it all the time...

but things have changed.

I spend my time
doing things I used to love.

Sometimes I sit quietly,
sometimes I just let the day pass
without overthinking everything.

I don't rush to check my phone anymore.

I don't wait
the way I used to.

Life feels simple now...

not empty,
just calm.

And slowly,
I'm getting used to this version of me.

I didn’t think of you
while painting this time.

During the day,
everything feels fine.

I stay busy,
I don't think much...
and it feels like
I've moved on.

But at night,
when everything gets quiet...
the thoughts come back.

Not as loud as before,
but still there.
I don't fight them anymore.
I just let them be...
and slowly,
they pass.

Because now I know

not every thought
needs to stay.

I don't need
closure anymore.

I gave myself
the answers
you never did.

I don't wait
for things to change...

I changed.

I don't go back
to what hurt me...

no matter
how much I once loved it.

No questions,
no expectations...

Now, when I look back, it doesn't feel as heavy. It's just something that happened, something that changed me, but didn't break me. I don't miss it the way I used to, and I don't wait for it anymore.

I'm not searching for what I lost. I'm learning to appreciate what I still have myself, my peace, and the life in front of me.

And for the first time in a long while,
that feels enough.

Dear,

I know it felt like you wouldn't be okay without them. I know there were days when everything felt heavy, and you didn't understand how to move forward. But look at you now... you made it through all of that.

You didn't rush, you didn't pretend. You just kept going, even on the days when it felt impossible. And slowly, without even realizing it, you started healing.

You don't need to forget everything. You don't need to have all the answers. You just need to keep choosing yourself, the way you're doing right now.

And trust me, one day you'll notice it too
you'll smile without thinking,
you'll feel light again,
and it won't hurt the same anymore.

So if you're still in the middle of it...
keep going.

You're getting there,
and you're doing better than you think.

Dear reader,

If this book made you feel something... if even a single page felt like your own story, then it means more to me than you can imagine.

Writing these words was never just about telling a story, it was about sharing feelings that are often left unspoken. And if you found a part of yourself in it, then this journey was worth it.

If you'd like to share your thoughts, your story, or simply tell me how this book felt to you, I would truly love to hear from you.

You can reach me on Instagram @miss.peace91

Take care of yourself
and don't forget,
you deserve the same love
you give to others.

About the Author

Kashish Agrahari writes for the people who feel deeply but often stay silent about their emotions. Her words are inspired by heartbreak, healing, memories, and the journey of finding yourself again after difficult endings. Through *And Then I Let Go*, she hopes to remind readers that healing takes time, and no one is truly alone in what they feel.

This is her first book.

www.ingramcontent.com/pod-product-compliance
Ingram Content Group UK Ltd.
Pitfield, Milton Keynes, MK11 3LW, UK
UKHW040038200726
13845UKWH00054B/469

9 788198 612304